SHORT·SCEN
WALKS

PAUL HANNON

HILLSIDE PUBLICATIONS
20 Wheathead Crescent
Keighley
West Yorkshire
BD22 6LX

First Published 2009

ISBN 978 1 870141 96 3

The sketch maps are based on 1947 OS one-inch maps and earlier OS six-inch maps

Cover illustration: Burnsall
Back cover: Barden Tower
Page 1: Bolton Abbey
(Paul Hannon/Hillslides Picture Library)

Printed by Steffprint
Unit 5, Keighley Industrial Park
Royd Ings Avenue
Keighley
West Yorkshire
BD21 4DZ

CONTENTS

INTRODUCTION

Wharfedale is the most popular valley within the Yorkshire Dales National Park, due in part to its accessibility from the West Yorkshire cities of Leeds and Bradford and their surrounding towns. More importantly, the dale is famed for its natural beauty and characterful villages, starting points for countless great walks: this collection embraces the lower dale from Burnsall and Appletreewick through Barden and Bolton Abbey. Upstream of Linton and Grassington the upper dale, featuring equally delightful countryside through Kettlewell and Buckden, is the subject of a companion guide to 20 further walks.

Between Grassington and Bolton Bridge the River Wharfe flows through an extraordinarily colourful and enchanting landscape, fusing limestone delights at Trollers Gill and Loup Scar with the gritstone bastions of Barden Moor and Fell, featuring the rocky crest of Simon's Seat amid rolling heather moors. At the heart of this is the Bolton

Barden Bridge

Abbey estate, focal point being the great priory ruins in a memorable riverside setting. Adjacent is stunning Strid Wood enveloping a lively section of the Wharfe, at the start of which is historic Barden Tower. Burnsall boasts one of the finest village settings in England, while lesser known delights include Beamsley, with its almshouses and moorland peak, and the quieter charms of Appletreewick, featuring Barben Beck and Skyreholme.

A number of the walks take advantage of Open Access, principally on the Barden Fell and Barden Moor access areas: these may be closed on certain days during the grouse shooting season (not Sundays) and at times of high fire risk. Notices are posted at the access points, but for advance information contact Grassington National Park Centre. Dogs are not allowed on the access areas. Most of these walks can be reached by an infrequent bus service through Bolton Abbey and Burnsall. Whilst the route description should be sufficient to guide you around each walk, a map is recommended for greater information: Ordnance Survey 1:25,000 scale maps give the finest detail, and Explorers OL2 and OL297 cover all the walks.

USEFUL INFORMATION

·Yorkshire Dales National Park
Colvend, Hebden Road, Grassington, Skipton BD23 5LB
(01756-752748)
·Grassington National Park Centre (01756-752774)
·Skipton Tourist Information (01756-792809)
·Ilkley Tourist Information (01943-602319)
·Yorkshire Dales Society (01729-825600)
(working to protect the area's natural beauty)
·Ramblers' Association
2nd Floor, Camelford House, 87-89 Albert Embankment,
London SE1 7BR (020-7339 8500)
·Traveline - public transport information (0870-6082608)

LOWER WHARFEDALE

20 Short Scenic Walks

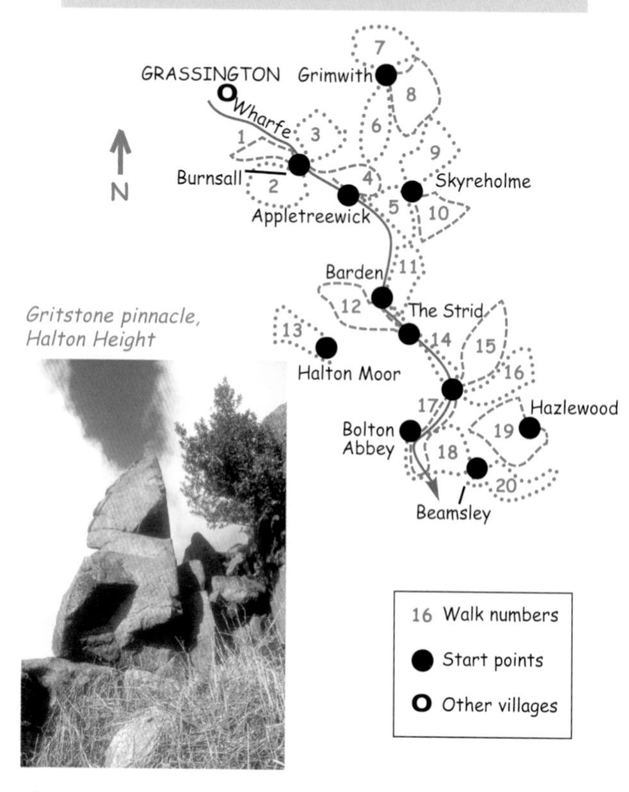

Gritstone pinnacle, Halton Height

A RECORD OF YOUR WALKS

WALK	DATE	NOTES
1		
2		
3		
4		
5		
6		
7		
8		
9		
10		
11		
12		
13		
14		
15		
16		
17		
18		
19		
20		

1 THORPE IN THE HOLLOW

3½ miles
from Burnsall

Riverbank, fieldpaths and a hidden hamlet in the shadow of Burnsall Fell

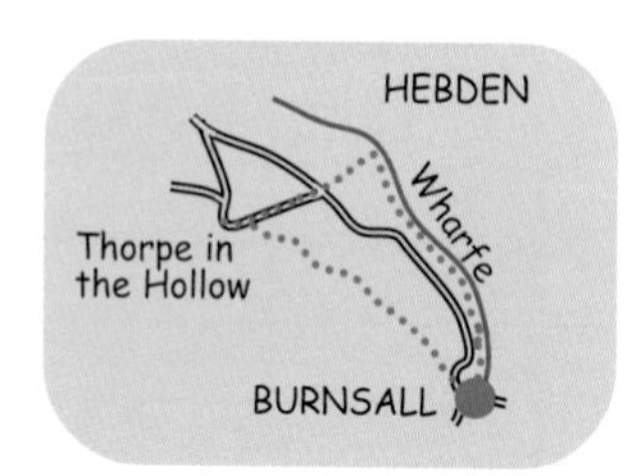

Start Village centre (GR: 032611), car park and seasonal field
Map OS Explorer OL2, Yorkshire Dales South/West

Burnsall's setting is one of near-perfection, with river, bridge, green, maypole, church, Red Lion pub and cottages forging a classic Wharfedale scene. St Wilfred's church dates largely from the 15th century, alongside is the lovely school, founded in 1602 as a grammar school. There is a second pub, the Devonshire Fell, shop, tearoom and WC. From the bridge turn upstream on the village side of the riverbank into fine surrounds. Passing beneath the rear of the upper village the river soon leads away, and the path rises to a knoll to look down on the gorge of Loup Scar, a very lively section of the Wharfe. Dropping back to the river, this leads delightfully upstream to the suspension bridge beneath Hebden. Though the walk doesn't cross it, this is a place to linger. It was constructed in 1885 to replace stepping-stones (Hebden Hippings) that have since been restored immediately downstream.

Leave by a bridle-gate on the left just before the bridge, and a steep path climbs the little bank. After looking back over this scene the path rises more gently away. From a gate at the top it runs faintly on the wallside heading away, through two further gates. By the time the brow is reached there are good views updale beyond Grass Wood. Continue on to a gate onto the B6160. Across is an old stone guidepost, with hands pointing to Burnsall, Linton and Kilnsey. Cross straight over onto the minor Thorpe Lane, leading to Thorpe. On the highest point the Burnsall path is signed off as a walled track on the left, but first advance two minutes further for a look at Thorpe. This farming hamlet has an elusiveness that allegedly kept it hidden from marauding Scots. Romantically titled Thorpe in the Hollow it shelters between reef knolls and below the overpowering Thorpe Fell. Note the little enclosed green.

Returning to the brow, take the signed path off through a gate and away as a walled track. Part way on it becomes more of a green footway as it drops down. Just five paces before it ends take a stile on the right, and drop down to a bridle-gate at the far end. Head away outside a small wood, and on with the wall to a stile at the end. Across the trickle behind, rise up the low bank and away again, crossing straight over two fields. Head across the centre of the next field, angling to the wall on the left to find, at the far end, a stile onto stony Badger Lane. Cross straight over and resume to a small brow, revealing Burnsall ahead. The church tower makes a useful guide, while Simon's Seat dominates the skyline behind.

Drop to a stile below, slant right to one in the bottom corner, then march in a straight line towards the village, a string of stiles pointing the way infallibly back. Burnsall Fell looks rugged up above, more so as the end is neared. Another stony track is crossed near the end, past which cross the last two fields to a gate into a tiny snicket onto the village street. Turn right for the green.

Loup Scar

2 BURNSALL FELL

4¾ miles
from Burnsall

The steep slopes hovering above the village lead to an exploration of a fine heathery moortop

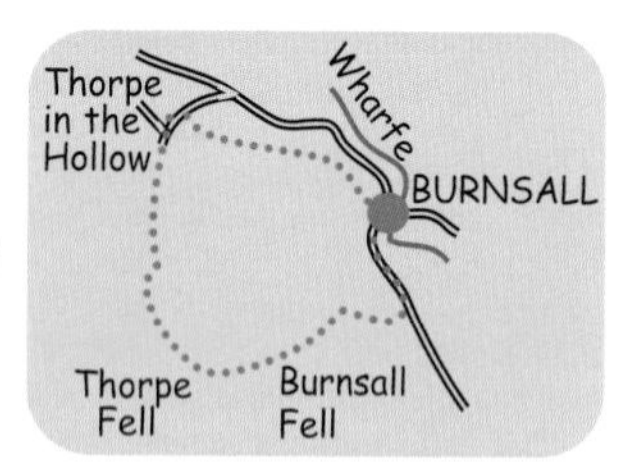

Start *Village centre (GR: 032611), car park and seasonal field*
Map *OS Explorer OL2, Yorkshire Dales South/West*
Access *Open Access land, no dogs: see page 5*

For a note on Burnsall see page 8. From the green go left in front of the Red Lion, and after the road swings right, a small gate on the left sends a snicket into a field. Head away, crossing a couple of wall-stiles to a track. Cross this to resume a direct line, encountering a string of stiles in parallel limestone walls. Burnsall Fell looms darkly to your left. When the pattern is broken slant right up to a stile in a crooked wall, rising over a brow to drop onto a track, Badger Lane. Head away again, crossing a large pasture to a stile at the far end, then on to another. Continue, dropping to a plank bridge then rising outside a wood. Keep on to a stile at the top, onto the end of a green lane. Go left on this, rising to run out onto a back road, where go left into Thorpe (see page 9).

Bear left in the centre and on to the road end. Take the left track climbing between walls to a gate onto the open moor. Of several sunken tracks heading away take the right-most one, directly ahead. It swings up to the right to terminate at the site of a small quarry. From a small cairn go left past its near side to broaden into a more substantial path, soon running level to the beginnings of Hesker Gill. Across, keep to the broad, left-hand way whose groove rises gently to quickly reach a fork at a small cairn and a few rocks. Bear right to rise up a gentle slope, soon reforming into one final sunken section. As the groove fades a stone shooting house appears ahead, and a firm track is joined just before it. At 1476ft/450m this is the walk's summit: a lesser hut below it offers refuge.

Turn left on the track for a quarter-mile down to a fork. Take the level, left branch, curving further left. Quickly swinging back right, take a thin trod rising left from a second tiny cairn 30 yards after a first, soon gaining a real cairn on scattered boulders. From here a thin trod heads away: forking within five yards, take the right branch. It declines gently, becoming clearer as you see a substantial cairn lower down. Improving further, the path gravitates to a more defined edge with a first view of Burnsall, and runs down above a few outcrops to the cairn. The six-foot beacon of Burnsall Fell occupies a bouldery plinth, the walk's finest moment. Its view covers much of Wharfedale, up to Great Whernside and across to closer features such as Appletreewick and Simon's Seat. The prize however is at your feet, for the bird's-eye view of Burnsall is unsurpassed!

Leave by an initially thin path dropping right above the declining bouldery edge. Becoming clearer it swings left, more directly down before narrowing to reach a substantial cairn above steeper ground. The path slants right, then left down a groove, with Air Scar Crags over to the right. The path quickly swings left as a super green way slanting into bracken. Just short of the intake wall it swings right to join and follow it right, to the far end of a plantation where a stile takes you off the moor into trees. Take the path running briefly left along the wood top before it drops onto a broadening green way to emerge onto the B6160. Turn left down to the village.

Burnsall from Burnsall Fell

3 AROUND LANGERTON HILL

4 miles
from Burnsall

An absorbing mixture of fieldpaths on the slopes above Burnsall, with some excellent all-round views

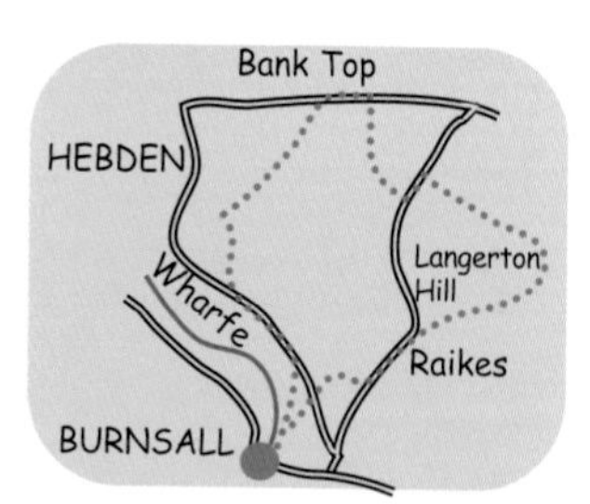

Start Village centre (GR: 032611), car park and seasonal field
Map OS Explorer OL2, Yorkshire Dales South/West

For a note on Burnsall see page 8. Leave by crossing the bridge and using steps on the left to descend to the Wharfe. Head upstream, the path soon becoming enclosed at a stile to run by the Wharfe until deflected in to a ladder-stile by a wall. Here the path forks: your return route descends the steep bank ahead, but for now bear left to slant up above the wooded bank of the river. Crossing a fence-stile a super path traverses above the wooded bank, looking across the river to Burnsall backed by Burnsall Fell. At the end it swings round to a stile onto narrow Skuff Road.

Go left on here for a while, as far as a stile on the right as the road bends and starts to drop. Cross the field, slanting right to a step-stile onto Ranelands' drive. Follow this right to the farm, and entering the yard take a gate left of the house. Back into a field, a thin path crosses to the far side where a wall-stile awaits by a gateway. From one just behind it you overlook Hebden Beck. Don't drop down but turn right on the wallside and rise to a gate at the top, by a barn. Continue climbing to a small gate in the top corner, virtually the end of the climbing. Rise to a wall-stile above then left to another just behind. Now rise up the field centre to cross to a stile by a gate in the far wall, with Bank Top farm behind. Cross the field centre to a ladder-stile onto the B6265.

Follow this right, past the farm and along a little further to the next farm, Hebden Moor Side. Pass into the yard between the buildings and from a gate to the left enter the field in front. Follow the wall down to gate in the far corner, then slant up to a ladder-stile in the facing wall. Now cross to a gate just beneath a barn to join the Hartlington Raikes road. Turn briefly left on here. Ahead, Great Whernside overtops the nearer moors, with Grimwith dam also distinctive. Drop down to quickly reach a wall-stile on the right. Descend the wallside to a stile at the bottom, then bear left down to one in the far corner. Head away with a wall on your right (Holes Beck is over the other side) to a stile by a corrugated barn, then on again to a stile accessing a path junction above a footbridge on the beck amid new tree plantings.

Cross the bridge and the stile behind and ascend the field, merging with the wall to reach a ladder-stile in it on the brow. Resume along the other side to a stile ahead under the crest of Langerton Hill. Continue away, the Barden Moor skyline returning as you pass through another stile and drop down in the same line, one further stile before advancing to one back onto the road at Raikes Farm. Turn left down the road a short way then take a stile on the right. Cross to one down near the corner and go left to another to reveal a fine view over the village. Drop to a stile back onto Skuff Road, crossing to another to make the steep drop to the outward route at the bottom stile, moving slowly to savour the spectacular views of village and fell.

The village school and church, Burnsall

4 — Wharfe below Burnsall

3¾ miles
from Burnsall

Hilly limestone pastures with wide open views sandwiched between some lovely riverside walking

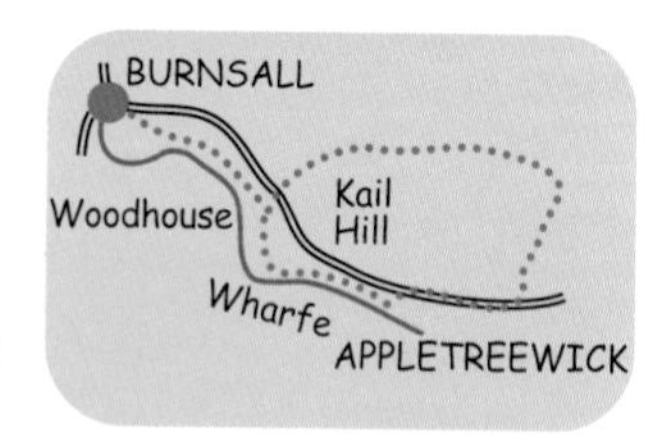

Start *Village centre (GR: 032611), car park and seasonal field*
Map *OS Explorer OL2, Yorkshire Dales South/West*

For a note on Burnsall see page 8. Leave by crossing the Wharfe on the graceful bridge, and quickly turning right through a gate/stile into a big riverside pasture. A path forms to run past a WC to a defined bank above the returning river, and the now firm path enjoys a lovely walk downstream. At a stile leave the Wharfe and cross the field towards the farm at Woodhouse. A footbridge takes you over Barben Beck onto the farm drive. Here forsake the river for now (you will return to this point) and turn left on the drive's short run out to a back road. Cross straight over to a gate/stile and head up an inviting sunken way. Soon a wall forms on the left and is followed all the way up on this green track, at the top becoming walled to run along to modern barns. On your left throughout this is the deep, tree-lined course of Barben Beck.

Left of the barns follow their access track up between walls, emerging to ascend a fieldside to a gate marking a path crossroads. Continue straight up the once-again walled track to a gate at the top to emerge into open pasture. Here forsake the track and rise to the wall corner just above, then follow the top side of the wall away to a stile in it just short of the corner. Before reaching this point the Barden Fell skyline of Simon's Seat and Earl Seat looks splendid ahead. Drop down the small field (ignore a ladder-stile on the left) to a wall-stile at the bottom, then down the wallside as far as a fine stile set into it. Resume on the other side of the wall until near the end, then cross the slim pasture to a tumbledown stile in an old wall and slant down to a gateway in the bottom corner. A track then runs down the short way to a gate at the head of an enclosed way to drop charmingly down onto the road at the top of Appletreewick. You emerge alongside the simple church of St John the Baptist, with imposing High Hall opposite.

Turn right to descend the street along the full length of the village. Appletreewick has several claims to fame, though many visitors best remember its delightful name. Three old halls and two pubs sit amongst a wonderful assortment of cottages. Probably the oldest is curiously named Mock Beggar Hall, a fine little edifice that once went by the title of Monk's Hall. The New Inn achieved national fame thanks to the enterprising 'no-smoking' policy of a 1970s landlord, while the Craven Arms boasts a superbly rebuilt cruck-framed barn - the village stocks stand outside. Continue past Low Hall to locate an enclosed path leading past a campsite to the river. Turn right to follow the Wharfe upstream. On emerging from trees the river takes a big swing to the left, and here the path is deflected right by an intervening wall to enter the farmyard at Woodhouse. This 17th century manor house boasts an attractive mullioned windowed frontage in an equally enviable setting. Passing to the right you reach the point you left early in the walk, so go straight ahead to the footbridge and retrace the opening half-mile.

The Wharfe below Woodhouse

5 AROUND APPLETREEWICK

3½ miles
from Appletreewick

Exceptional river scenery and much of interest in and around the environs of Skyreholme

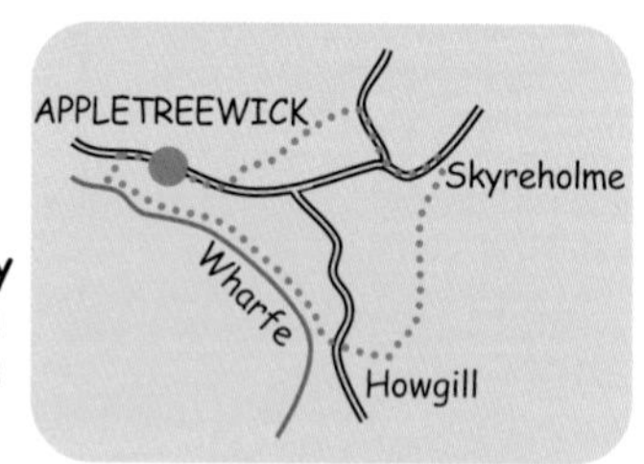

Start Village centre (GR: 053601), limited roadside parking, with seasonal field parking near the river
Map OS Explorer OL2, Yorkshire Dales South/West

For a note on Appletreewick see page 15. Leave by heading west on the Burnsall road, past the two pubs and Low Hall to reach a walled path leading past a campsite to the Wharfe. Turn left alongside the river, meeting an early interruption as a steep, wooded bank deflects the path up wooden steps before returning more steadily to the riverbank. Now the Wharfe is faithfully adhered to through open pastures. Simon's Seat rises ahead, with Burnsall Fell across the river. At the end you enter a delightfully wooded section. Emerging via a bridle-gate at its far end, note the simple but touching memorial plate affixed to a rock. Forsaking the river the path bears left across a field to reach a gate pointing out onto a narrow road at a bridge on Fir Beck at Howgill.

Cross the bridge and leave the road in favour of an enclosed track up to the left. Beyond a nice cottage it narrows to meet Howgill Lane at the top, alongside the farm at Howgill. Turn left along the unsurfaced lane past the caravan site at Howgill Lodge, where refreshments may be available. Just a little beyond a converted barn note an old milestone set into the wall: it points the way to 'Patley Bridge 6', indicating the lane's once greater importance. At this point leave by a gate opposite and follow an old green way along the wallside, first on its right, then its left. After a gateway, with Skyreholme straight ahead, slope down to a stile in the next wall, and continue down to cross a tiny beck at an old wall. With Skyreholme Beck just to the left advance along the field to a footbridge on it. Just before this a well-preserved limekiln stands across to the right. Over the bridge suburban steps ascend to a housing development to emerge onto the road at Skyreholme.

Turn left as far as a T-junction alongside an old chapel, then double back right, steeply uphill. This stiff pull gives chance to look back to Simon's Seat looming over Skyreholme before easing out on passing a barn. Just past it take a stile on the left and slant away down the field, quickly revealing a gap-stile in the wall below. This is the first of a sustained string of such gap-stiles, indeed the next few can be discerned ahead. All you do is simply be guided by these on a steady slant down across the fields towards the edge of Appletreewick. At the bottom cross a moist dip alongside an old wall, and rise up the gentle brow behind to a redundant gap-stile in a short length of wall. All that remains is a direct march across some narrow pastures with stiles in line, emerging at the end by one final squeezer-stile onto an enclosed track. Go left on this to emerge between houses onto the road at the top of Appletreewick. Alongside is the simple church of St John the Baptist, opposite is the imposing High Hall with its mullioned and transomed windows.

The Wharfe at Appletreewick

6 ABOVE BARBEN BECK

4¾ miles
from Grimwith

The lovely side valley of Barben Beck leads to good tracks over gently rolling hills with open views

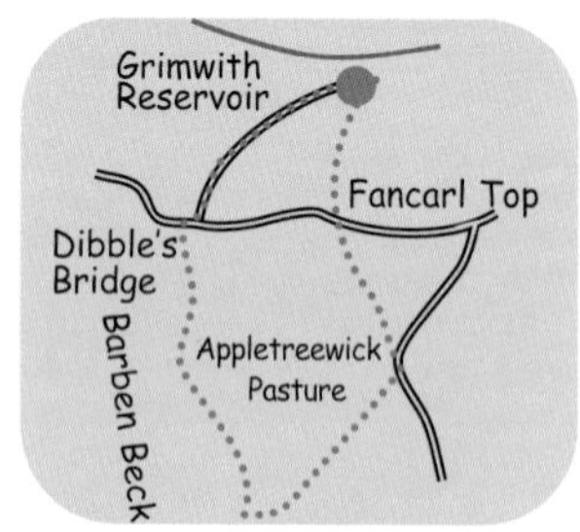

Start Grimwith Reservoir (GR: 062640), water company car park
Map OS Explorer OL2, Yorkshire Dales South/West

Surrounded by rolling moorland, Grimwith Reservoir was constructed in 1884 to supply water to Bradford, and substantial enlargement in 1983 made it the largest expanse of inland water in Yorkshire. Improved access has seen the provision of car park, WC and quiet water sports facilities. Start by following the access road back out through open surrounds onto the B6265. Turn right down to the steep dip at Dibble's Bridge. This was the scene of a tragic coach crash in 1975, when Britain's worst motoring disaster resulted in 32 fatalities. Between the reservoir and the bridge the watercourse is the River Dibb: covering only one mile under this guise, is it the shortest river in the country? Immediately below the bridge the Dibb becomes Barben Beck, across which is a lovely solitary house, a former mill.

Without crossing the bridge turn downstream through a gate, giving access to a beckside area of limestone outcrops, a long abandoned quarry. Vacate it by a stile in the far top corner, and slant up to a gate ahead. Continue straight across to a stile at the far end to enter the untamed expanse of Appletreewick Pasture sloping down to Barben Beck. Dropping to cross a tiny beck, note the large boulder alongside: it contains several cup marks, Bronze Age relics of uncertain purpose. The thin path slants up a little before commencing a long, level section on an intermittent route high above the attractive beck.

When a wall appears in front, deflect left of it to find converging walls at the top end. Escape along a narrow passage on the left. During this brief section you bridge an old stone arch, the site of a tunnel used during 18th century lead mining operations. On emerging turn right and remain with the wall, through a gate then a stile before ultimately joining an enclosed track at a path cross-roads. Turn left here on the initially walled track, rising away from a gate at the top to slant left up open pasture to a gate in the wall above. Through this the going eases out to cross the broad swathe of Appletreewick Pasture, with views dominated by Simon's Seat. The track runs unfailingly along to a gate onto New Road.

Turn left the short way to a bend, and here take a gate/stile on your left. A green track heads away with the wall all the way along to the far end, noting the gnarled rocks of Fancarl Crag to your right. Becoming enclosed the track runs a short course out back onto the B6265 at Fancarl Top. Cross straight over and head off along a windswept moorland track offering a sweeping panorama over Wharfedale to the mass of Barden Moor. As Grimwith Road it was the access road to the farms of Grimwith House and Gate Up, either abandoned or drowned by the arrival of the deep waters. It leads unfailingly and rapidly back to the start.

High summer above Barben Beck, looking to Barden Moor

7 GRIMWITH RESERVOIR

4¼ miles
from Grimwith

An uncomplicated circuit of a vast sheet of water, its moorland surrounds adding a sense of space and colour

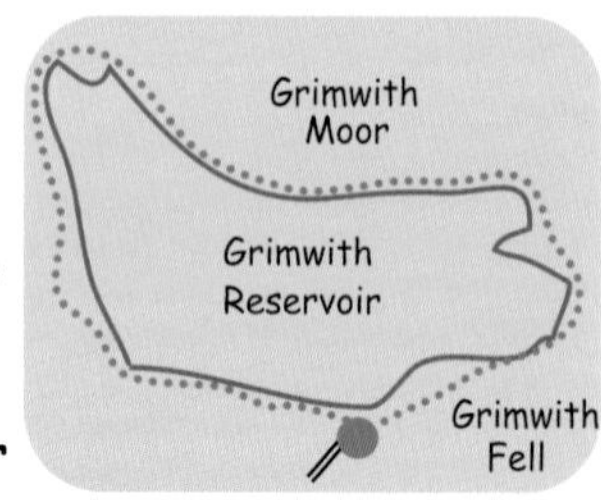

Start Grimwith Reservoir (GR: 062640), water company car park
Map OS Explorer OL2, Yorkshire Dales South/West

Grimwith Reservoir was constructed in 1884 to supply water to Bradford, and substantial enlargement in 1983 made it the largest expanse of inland water in Yorkshire. The old footpath encircling it had to be replaced, though in the great drought of 1995 we completed this walk on what could have been the original path, such was the absence of water. Improved public access has seen the provision of car park, WC and quiet water sports facilities. Grimwith is surrounded by rolling moorlands, and in late summer the purple heather makes a fine backdrop.

From the car park head east along the track rising away, with the sailing club below. Beyond a gate the wall drops away, after which an inviting path branches off left, slanting down the heathery bank to run above the shoreline. At the end it rejoins the track at High Laithe Barn, a cruck-framed and heather-thatched

listed building. Resume along the hard track past the farm buildings of Grimwith House and a side dam where Grimwith Beck comes in. The track winds round past a shooting house up to the right and the ruin of Gate Up on the left. Evidence of mullioned windows suggests that long ago this was a house of character. Looking across the reservoir, over the dam is the Barden Moor skyline.

When the track finally turns to climb to a barn, keep straight on a broad path through bracken to the far corner of the reservoir. This is the finest section as it passes along the foot of two attractive side gills, Gate Up Gill and Blea Gill. During the 1995 drought the stone bridge beneath where these two met stood uncovered, a curiously isolated structure amid sun-baked peat. The path emerges from the 'far corner' and its bracken as a track returns, leading down the west side now. There are grand views back into Gate Up Gill and the Grimwith and Appletreewick Moors: ahead, beyond the dam, Simon's Seat breaks the skyline. At a fork the return path is sent down to the left, past a barn and then on as a broader walled track to reach the western end of the great dam. A pleasant walk along the top of the relatively unobtrusive grassy embankment leads back to the road just short of the car park.

Left: High Laithe

Grimwith 'Reservoir' in the 1995 drought: a resurrected bridge in the sun-baked peat

8 NURSERY KNOT

$4\frac{3}{4}$ miles
from Grimwith

An invigorating ramble on good paths and tracks across wild uplands leading to a limestone landmark

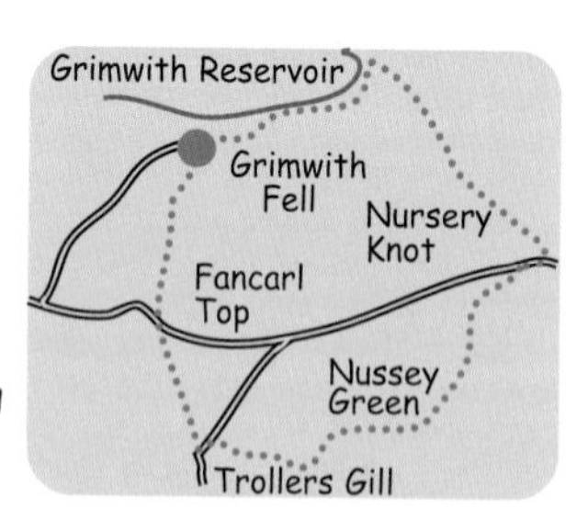

Start Grimwith Reservoir (GR: 062640), water company car park
Map OS Explorer OL2, Yorkshire Dales South/West
Access Open Access land (not grouse moors)

For a note on Grimwith see page 20. From the car park turn up the drive between the WC and houses, and from the gate above, a windswept moorland track heads away with a sweeping panorama over Wharfedale to Barden Moor. Meeting the B6265 at Fancarl Top, cross over onto a green lane, soon losing an enclosing wall to run an idyllic course to join New Road on a bend. Simon's Seat rises ahead, while close by to your left are the boulders of Fancarl Crag. Go briefly left on the road to a stile on the right, and beyond a few reeds a green path heads away past a circular pool, dropping gently to join a grassy old mine track. Before reaching it, note the dark slit entrance to Hell Hole just down to the left. Turn right on the old track just as far as a bend, where fork left on an inviting permissive path linking to Open Access land. It makes a short pull before crossing the neck of land to drop down to cross a stile and stream in the upper valley of Trollers Gill. The ravine itself is along to the right, and can easily be visited (see WALK 9).

Your route is left, a path slanting up from the beck to a spoil heap and ruined hut at a lead mining site. Behind the hut is the arched entrance of a mine level. Here a superb green track starts to climb away. To the left note the breached wall of an old dam, while higher up some scattered rocks to the left bear cup marks of

Bronze Age people. This delectable track rises steadily up the open country of Nussey Green to a gate at the top, joining the firm track of Black Hill Road. Turn left along here, (with Nursery Knot directly ahead) dropping steadily towards Dry Gill to meet the B6265.

Turn right along the verge for a few minutes to the foot of a steep pull to Stump Cross Caverns, and a path leaves the road at a pocket of open ground on the left. After a stile it shakes off its accompanying wall and rises across grassy moor to the foot of Nursery Knot. While the path passes to its right, a left branch takes a closer look. At 1276ft/389m the limestone knoll of Nursery Knot is the summit of the walk, with sweeping views across the reservoir to Great Whernside. At the wall corner below, two adjacent stiles can be taken in tandem before the path heads off over several rough pastures: occasional stakes point towards Grimwith Reservoir.

Through an old wall the path drops towards the end of a large enclosure, but takes a stile in the left-hand wall before the end to continue its slant. A near pathless, moist pasture is followed by a dry, reedy one before passing beneath an island barn in the first of a couple of green fields to join a rough road alongside the reservoir. Turn left to pass the cruck-framed, heather-thatched High Laithe Barn (see page 20). Here go right on a more inviting path which runs on the heathery slope before rising to rejoin the hard track, with the start just a couple of minutes further.

Grimwith Reservoir

9 TROLLERS GILL

3 miles
from Skyreholme

A hidden limestone ravine is centrepiece to a very easy ramble amid much further interest and views

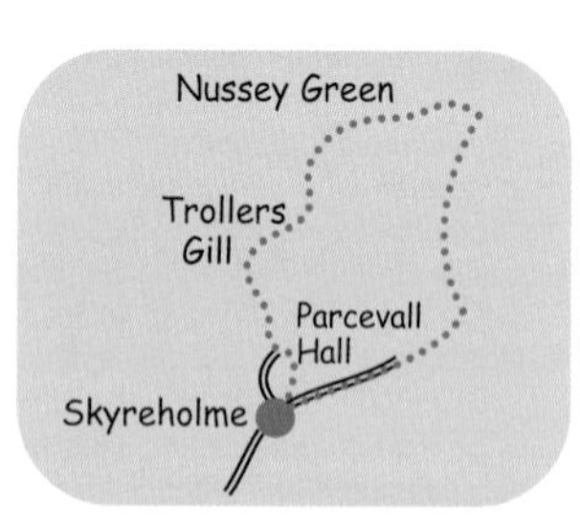

Start Middle Skyreholme (GR: 068607), limited parking at bridge, also limited space on road to Parcevall Hall
Map OS Explorer OL2, Yorkshire Dales South/West
Access Open Access land (not grouse moors)

Skyreholme is a scattered farming hamlet in its own side valley beneath the dark wall of Simon's Seat. From the junction at the phone box and seat, cross the bridge and take a small gate on the left to ascend to a gateway at the top corner. Now cross the field to another gateway, keeping on with a wall to a corner stile at Ridge End House, and also a tearoom. On your right is the entrance to Parcevall Hall, Upper Wharfedale's grandest house. Built over 300 years ago, its beautiful stonework looks across to Simon's Seat. Now a diocesan retreat centre, the gardens and woodland are open to the public from Easter to October (fee payable).

Go left over the wooden bridge onto the public road-end, and take a gate on the right to follow Skyreholme Beck upstream on a good path through more gates. A stile beyond a barn admits to Open Country, and this colourful enclosure features the grassy retaining wall of a reservoir. Made to serve mills at Skyreholme, all are now history. Beyond another stile the path forks in the amphitheatre just short of Trollers Gill, split by the high wedge of Middle Hill. Opt for the right branch, this being the main path which curves into the more open, stony surrounds which only at the last moment reveal the secretive entrance to Trollers Gill. Though not particularly tall, the cliffs of this magnificent limestone gorge remain virtually unbroken for some distance, and the slim passage between is usually dry. It is renowned as the home of the legendary 'Barguest', a spectral hound with eyes like saucers.

Emerging, simply continue along the shallow trough, the stream probably re-appearing before you reach a stile further on. Just past it, ignore a stile across the stream and advance on, the path slanting up from the beck to a spoil heap and ruined hut at a former lead mining site. Behind the hut is the arched entrance of an old mine level. Here a super green track starts to climb away. To the left note the breached wall of an old dam, while higher up some of the scattered rocks to the left bear cup marks of Bronze Age people (including a flat boulder sporting a dozen distinctive scoops). This delectable track rises steadily up the open country of Nussey Green to a gate in the wall at the top, joining the firmer surface of Black Hill Road. Turn right on here, the track running for some time along to a junction with another walled way. Turn right down here, becoming surfaced to descend Skyreholme Bank. Glorious views look across the Skyreholme valley to Simon's Seat before you are returned to the start.

The entrance to Trollers Gill

10 Simon's Seat

4 miles
from Skyreholme

A real fellwalk to a celebrated landmark that frowns benevolently over the Skyreholme scene

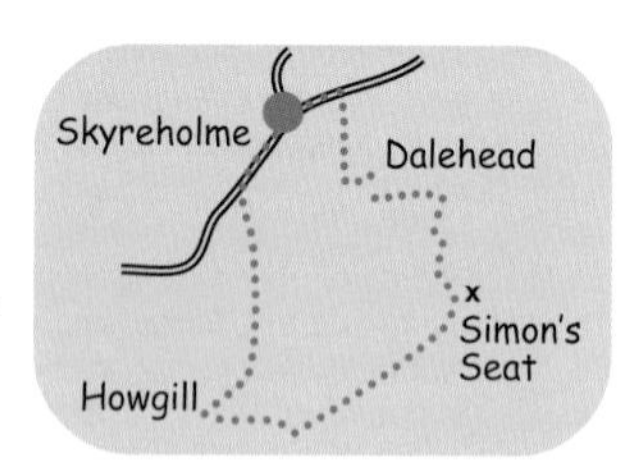

Start Middle Skyreholme (GR: 068607), limited parking at bridge, also limited space on road to Parcevall Hall
Map OS Explorer OL2, Yorkshire Dales South/West
Access Open Access land, no dogs: see page 5

From the junction at the phone box and seat, cross the bridge and head up the ascending road, Skyreholme Bank. Towards the end of a small cluster of dwellings, take a gate into the yard of the last two. Drop down between them to a small gate into a field, then slant down to a footbridge in the corner. Rise away bearing right to a wall-stile, and on again past a wall corner to a stile at a barn. Just beyond is a gate onto a walled farm road, Howgill Lane.

Turn briefly left, and before reaching Dalehead Farm a gate on the right points a permissive path towards Simon's Seat. As height is gained, fine views unfold over the Skyreholme scene. Slanting right through bracken it crosses a fence-stile to double back right. It then quickly doubles back left for a sustained, part sunken slant to the top of scattered trees. With tree planting in evidence, turn right up an initially sunken way which quickly doubles back left to commence another sustained slant, mostly sunken amid heather. Keep faith with this as it finally performs an acute hairpin back up to the right: you'll quickly see the not too-distant summit rocks directly above. The path winds fairly directly up to a gate/stile in a sturdy wall. The summit is now only a short strike above, and the path rises steadily right before ascending more directly over gentler ground to near the rocks. A stone-flagged ascent climbs steeply past the edge of the rocks to the moortop.

Advance towards a detached group of large rocks, noting these for your departure. To gain the summit double back left, picking up a path running to just beyond the highest rocks, where hands are required for the final few feet. At 1591ft/485m an OS column adorns the top: the view features a wide sweep of the Dales, including Fountains Fell, Buckden Pike and Great Whernside. At your feet is a bird's-eye view of Skyreholme and Appletreewick, featuring Trollers Gill, Parcevall Hall and Grimwith Reservoir.

Leave by dropping back onto the path heading south, but bear right to the left edge of the detached group, where a firm path heads away on a gradual descent. Meeting a wall to drop down alongside it, a track merges near the end to enter an access strip off the fell. A broad path descends between plantations, opening out towards the bottom to drop down onto unsurfaced Howgill Lane by the farm at Howgill. Turn right on it past a caravan site at Howgill Lodge, where refreshments may be available. Beyond a converted barn, a milestone in the wall points to 'Patley Bridge 6', indicating the lane's once greater importance. Leave by a gate opposite and follow an old wallside green way, first on its right, then its left. After a gateway slope down to a stile in the next wall, and down to cross a tiny beck at an old wall. With Skyreholme Beck to the left advance along the field to cross a footbridge on it. Suburban steps ascend to housing to emerge onto the road at Skyreholme. Turn right to finish, passing attractive Lane House Farm.

Simon's Seat

11 UNDER EARL SEAT

4¼ miles
from Barden

Delectable riverside walking precedes a stiff pull to the edge of the moors

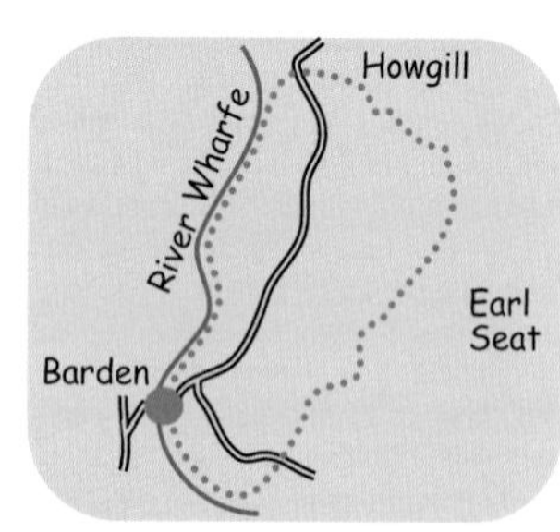

Start Barden Bridge (GR: 052573), roadside and seasonal Barden Field car park
Map OS Explorer OL2, Yorkshire Dales South/West or Explorer 297, Lower Wharfedale/Washburn Valley
Access Open Access land, no dogs: see page 5

Barden boasts the Wharfe's finest bridge: a tablet dates its restoration 'at the charge of the whole West Riding' as 1676. Just up the hill is the imposing Barden Tower. Built as a hunting lodge by the powerful Cliffords of Skipton Castle, it boasted two famous residents from that family. Henry the 'Shepherd' Lord came in 1485, preferring Barden's peace to Skipton's splendour: he had the adjacent chapel built. The redoubtable Lady Anne restored the Tower in 1659 and spent much of her final years here, a tablet survives to confirm her work. The chapel is now a restaurant.

From the parking area turn upstream with the Wharfe, a good path squeezing between river and road. As the latter rises away, take a gate set back on the left. A path rejoins the riverbank which is followed faithfully all the way upstream to Howgill. Every step is a delight, with open views on either side. The latter half is largely enclosed until the sidestream of Fir Beck deflects you away from the river, past a farm and out onto a back road at Howgill. Cross the road, not the bridge, and rise away on an enclosed track. Beyond a cottage it narrows to meet unsurfaced Howgill Lane at the top, alongside the farm at Howgill. Cross straight over to a gate to ascend a track that serves as a permissive path to the moor. After some open pasture it climbs more steeply between plantations to ultimately open out onto the moor beneath the unseen dome of Earl Seat.

Ignoring the broad path rising left, make for the right-hand wall corner and head away with the moor-foot wall enclosing the plantations. A gentle path makes a steady rise to a brow, after which a lengthy, level section follows along the base of dense heather flanks that rise to the bouldery 1473ft/449m crown of Earl Seat. Ultimately a steady descent starts as far as a corner where wall and trees drop away. Big views open out, down the valley backed by the Rombalds Moor skyline and across to Barden Moor cradling its lower reservoir. The path also turns to drop more sharply, and as the wall makes a big curve right the path drops onto a track. Bear right on it, quickly turning to descend pleasantly to a gate/stile in the wall below.

Alongside stands a stone inscribed BCWW, indicating the course of a pipeline built by Bradford Corporation Water Works; Barden Tower also comes into view to the right. The track continues down bracken-covered Cony Warren, with Barden Aqueduct seen below. A gate/stile at the bottom put you onto a back road alongside a cottage. Cross to a stile opposite and descend a permissive path to another stile in the bottom corner, then drop down the bank to the impressive stone aqueduct. All that remains is to turn upstream for the lovely walk back to Barden Bridge, which soon beckons ahead.

Wharfedale at Barden

12 — Barden Moor

4¾ miles from The Strid

A rewarding stroll through all things Barden, visiting bridge, tower, moor and reservoir

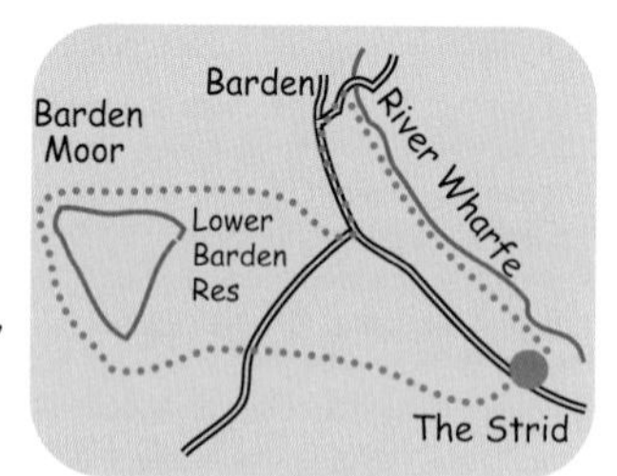

Start *The Strid (GR: 058563), car park*
Map *OS Explorer OL2, Yorkshire Dales South/West*
Access *Open Access land, no dogs: see page 5*

From the shop descend the access road to its side, past WCs and a cottage a firm carriageway drops into Strid Wood. Quickly reaching a fork, bear left on a slightly less broad path. The Strid itself (visited in Walk 14) is to the right, downstream. Continue your descent to the Wharfe's bank just below. Turn left, and within a minute you cross a footbridge to leave the wood. The firm path runs upstream, passing beneath the imposing Barden Aqueduct to reach Barden Bridge. Don't cross this magnificent structure, but take the road climbing steeply to Barden Tower. A stile in the wall gives access to the ruin, beyond which its entrance leads out onto the B6160. For more on Barden Tower see page 28.

Turn left along the main road just as far as the Embsay turning. Only two minutes up it, take a gate/stile on the right onto Barden Moor. A firm access track heads away, rising steadily through increasing heather towards the grassy dam of Lower Barden Reservoir. Ignoring a branch left towards the dam, continue straight up to run through bracken high above the shoreline. The whole reservoir is revealed, with the upper reservoir's dam on the skyline backed by Cracoe war memorial. Above the reservoir head the track meets a wall. Don't pass through but take a contrastingly slender path doubling back left down through the bracken. At the small dam it runs along the edge, over a stile and a footbridge to meet another hard track. Go left on this, a splendid moorland promenade with big views over the reservoir to Simon's Seat and Earl Seat. After absorbing a track from the embankment a crossroads is reached with a surfaced access road. Go straight across to imposing Broad Park House, and simply continue on the wallside track heading away. When the wall turns off remain on the near-level track to a gate back onto the Embsay road.

From a gate opposite follow a path across the bottom edge of moorland to a gate in a wall ahead. The path bears gently left on a generally level course across rough pasture. A moist tract around a stream is best tackled by bearing left to a couple of stunted oaks, crossing the marshiest environs where the stream drops steeply away. The path resumes at the other side to reach a wall corner, then on, intermittently green then wet, to a gate in the wall ahead. Don't pass through but ascend the wallside, reedy beginnings leading to a nice path rising to a brow. Look back from here to a big sweep of Barden Moor, with both tower and bridge featuring. The path then briefly traces a curving embankment before rejoining the wall, at which point take a stile in it and descend the wallside in the walk's only field. Part way down, a stone indicates the course of the Nidd Aqueduct pipeline built by Bradford Corporation Water Works. From a stile in the bottom corner join the B6160, with the start just yards to your right.

The chapel, Barden Tower

13 Halton Height

3¼ miles
from Halton Moor

A walk entirely on heather moorland, on a rocky fringe of Barden Moor peeping into the Aire Valley

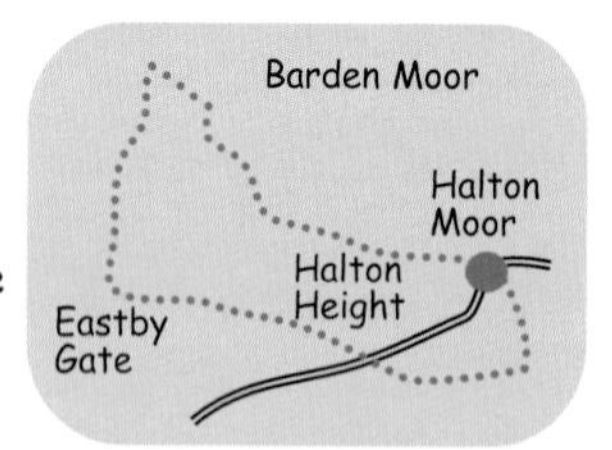

Start *Top of Embsay-Barden road (GR: 037554), lay-bys*
Map *OS Explorer OL2, Yorkshire Dales South/West*
Access *Open Access land, no dogs: see page 5*

The summit of the Embsay-Barden road is a very popular motorists' halt above the easternmost of two cattle-grids, enjoying priceless views over Lower Barden Reservoir to the majestic sweep of Simon's Seat and its moorland heights above the Wharfe. Don't cross the cattle-grid but turn right on a wallside track heading along the moor-edge, down through the little gulch of How Gill. Views ahead look to Beamsley Beacon and Rombalds Moor framing the lower reaches of Wharfedale. The track swings right to run to the head of grassy Moor Lane. Don't take the gate onto it but remain on a thin grassy path continuing along the foot of bracken-clad moor. This splendid little path shortly slants up beneath the boulders of Low Crag, short-cutting a bend of the wall to squeeze up between wall and edge back onto the moorland road.

Go briefly left, and before the cattle-grid turn up a grassy track on the right, parallel with the nearby wall enclosing woods. A distinctive pinnacle dominates the bouldery scene above. The track winds up to join the wall, but soon doubles sharply back right to rise to the base of an extensive old quarry at High Crag. Set back above this is an OS column and cairn at 1171ft/357m, the top of Halton Height. At the right end of the quarry rises the pinnacle (illustrated on page 6). Remain on the track as it runs left to expire beneath the far end of the cliff. A thin trod takes up the running, quickly levelling out to approach the wall again. Gaining the crest, views open out ahead to Embsay Crag and more of Barden Moor's great expanse. Simply trace this thin path close by the wall, dropping gently down to the gate/stile at Eastby Gate.

Turn sharp right here to remain on the moor, veering slightly left through a few reeds to locate a quickly forming grass path. This runs to the first of a row of grouse butts, with a broad grass track to the right also. At the end of the butts a broader way takes over. Ahead, more of the moor opens out with the lower reservoir outspread below, while Simon's Seat looms dramatically over Wharfedale. Slanting down to the right, the way quickly becomes a Landrover track dropping down to arrive between two shooters' cabins at Hutchen Gill Head.

Whilst an obvious short-cut simply follows this down to rapidly meet a firmer track, the Rylstone-Bolton Abbey bridleway, a nicer, short loop is to bear left past the second cabin, from where a short-lived trough leads to cross the breached dam of an old reservoir, then on a trod through heather and bilberry to quickly meet the firm track of the bridleway. Turn right on this, dropping down to absorb the shooters' track from the cabins, and your way leads across the moor under Halton Height. This relaxing stroll gives unlimited chance to fully absorb the spectacular views across the moor as it returns you unfailingly to the road at the start.

Lower Barden Reservoir and Simon's Seat from Barden Moor

14 STRID WOOD

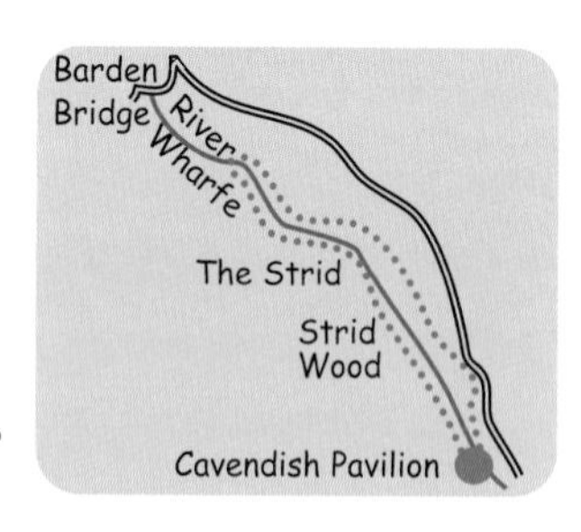

3¾ miles
from Bolton Abbey

Excellent paths through an outstanding blend of river and woodland, awesome in autumn colour

Start Cavendish Pavilion (GR: 077552), Sandholme car park
Map OS Explorer OL2, Yorkshire Dales South/West or Explorer 297, Lower Wharfedale/Washburn Valley

This delectable section of the Wharfe is part of the Duke of Devonshire's Bolton Abbey estate, and a combination of largely permissive paths allows good access to both banks. With the exception of the Pavilion to Posforth Bridge all paths remain private, though 'the public are invited to walk and picnic' in a style that captures the Victorian flavour still evident in some of the quainter touches hereabouts. The Pavilion offers all manner of refreshments, with a gift shop and WC alongside.

Other than at the Strid it is the woodland itself that steals the show from the river. Strid Wood is a hugely popular riverside habitat where man and nature appear to happily co-exist. The importance of the woodland for bird and plant life has been recognised by designation as a Site of Special Scientific Interest (SSSI) and this should be respected by keeping to the paths. This should not pose any problems, for a splendid network was laid out during the 19th century, being well-maintained ever since.

From the Pavilion cross the wooden bridge and turn upstream. At a stile into woodland the path forks: remain on the riverbank, quickly crossing a footbridge adjacent to the road bridge on Posforth Gill. The path clings to the river until faced with a surprisingly sustained pull to the top of the wood, where a well-sited rest house awaits. Bedecked with a luxuriant bilberry thatch, this up-market seat is the first of several well-chosen viewpoints. Hereafter easy walking ensues along a magnificent terrace. One particular glimpse gives a surprise cameo of the Strid, perfectly framed by foliage. Shortly afterwards comes another classic, as the High Strid is revealed in a contrastingly open setting. The path leaves the wood at a stile to descend to the riverbank at Barden Aqueduct. This impressive structure was built to carry a water pipeline from the Nidderdale reservoirs to the taps of Bradford: it also carries a path, so cross and set off on the return, downstream back into Strid Wood.

Remain on the main path, ignoring an early fork to the Strid car park (with refreshments, shop and WC), then rising and wending nicely along past a viewpoint seat (Barden Tower is visible upstream) with the High Strid on the river. After a steady pull to the wood top, take a branch left running above a rock pinnacle - the Hawkstone - to drop down to the famous Strid itself. This is the focal point of the wood, as the Wharfe is forced through a narrow gritstone channel of great depth. Lives have been lost in senseless attempts to leap the foaming waters. Beyond the Strid simply remain on the broad carriageway created for early visitors which leads gently back all the way to the Cavendish Pavilion, a couple of late branches offering closer spells with the river.

The Strid

15 — Valley of Desolation

4¼ miles
from Bolton Abbey

This delectable side valley makes a mockery of its name, and leads to a more open moorland return

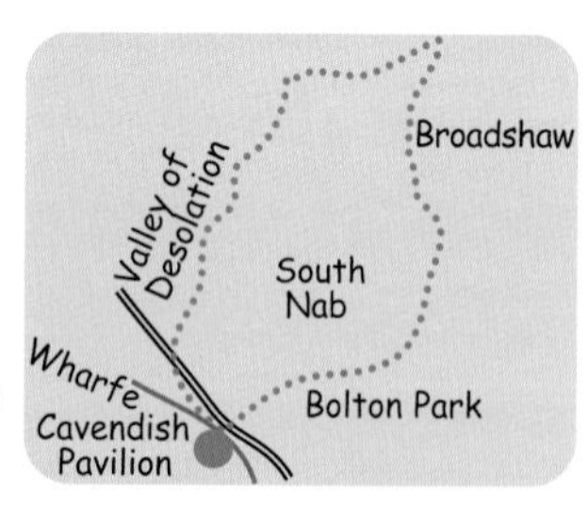

Start Cavendish Pavilion (GR: 077552), Sandholme car park
Map Explorer OL2, Yorkshire Dales South/West
or Explorer 297, Lower Wharfedale/Washburn Valley
Access Open Access land, no dogs: see page 5

The Cavendish Pavilion stands on the riverbank at the entrance to Strid Wood, with refreshments, gift shop and WC. Leave by crossing the wooden bridge over the Wharfe and taking a broad path upstream. Through a gate at the end the path forks: take the right branch climbing to a back road. Turn left up this a short way to its high point, where take a permissive path from a gate on the right. An inviting green track heads left past Waterfall Cottage to a gate, from where a firmer track winds along to fade alongside a pond, with Posforth Gill just in front in the Valley of Desolation. The title could not be less appropriate to the colourful terrain, but it refers to the aftermath of a great storm in 1826.

Turn right on a path forming to run along the rim of the steep drop to the beck, noting a cameo viewpoint for a beautiful waterfall. In summer this can be partly obscured by foliage, but the only alternative involves dropping to the beck earlier to wander upstream for a close-up view. The main path resumes high above the beck to quickly reach a footbridge on it. Across, it continues more narrowly along the valley floor, soon reaching a fork. While a brief diversion runs upstream to see another lovely waterfall, the main path rises left to a gate into Laund Pasture Plantation. A broad track ascends rapidly to the far end of the trees, where a gate admits into Open Country at a moorland corner. The dome of Earl Seat is on the left, with the Simon's Seat path distinct ahead.

Two good tracks head away: ignore that to the left, and take the delightful wallside one straight ahead. This is quickly left in favour of a more inviting green track bearing right to keep faith with the wall, dropping to cross Agill Beck to a gate/stile behind. An old stone trough sits on the grassy bank. After five minutes on the moor you leave Open Country, for now. Through the wall follow a gentle green track across a couple of pastures to the old barn of Agill House. Continue to a gateway beyond it and then a gate, from where a better track runs above tree-lined Hudson Gill. Dropping to a concrete crossing, the track doubles back up the other side to a gate. It runs on through a gateway and swings left with the wall to the old farm of Broadshaw in its very secluded location.

Pass between the buildings and follow the access track down to a ford and footbridge, then away over a brow and on to a cattle-grid to re-enter Open Country. Rising through heather the walk's summit is gained at some 1033ft/315m on Hammerthorn Hill. Extensive moorland leads the eye to Rombalds Moor, the South Pennines and Pendle Hill. The track drops to Hammerthorn Gate, meeting another track coming in from the left to leave the moor together. Through the gate continue down the stony track, with Bolton Priory seen in its delectable green setting on the valley floor. The track drops unfailingly down through the fields to the attractive farmhouse of Bolton Park. Passing to the right of the buildings its drive leads down to the back road, with just the bridge to re-cross to finish.

Waterfall in the Valley of Desolation

16 HAZLEWOOD MOOR

4½ miles
from Bolton Abbey

A very uncomplicated high level moorland circuit of Pickles Gill, on solid tracks throughout

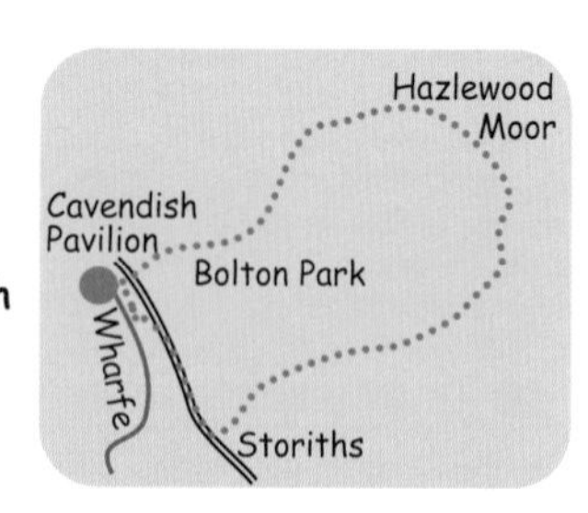

Start Cavendish Pavilion (GR: 077552), Sandholme car park
Map Explorer OL2, Yorkshire Dales South/West
or Explorer 297, Lower Wharfedale/Washburn Valley
Access Open Access land, no dogs: see page 5

The riverbank Cavendish Pavilion offers all manner of refreshments, with a gift shop and WC alongside. Cross the broad wooden bridge on the Wharfe and take the path downstream. At the far end of the pasture a stile/gate put you onto the parallel back road to negotiate Pickles Beck, with a footbridge upstream of the ford. Across, commence a stiff pull up the road to the hamlet of Storiths. Back o'th' Hill Farm in this unassuming settlement has refreshments and a model railway. On your left at the central junction is Storiths Crag, an outlying pocket of access land. Turn left onto it on a short-lived track past a cottage. It narrows to a path to rise up a wallside to meet a stony drive. Turn left on this to approach Town End Farm, then bear right over a cattle-grid onto open moor.

Already you have grand views, with a section of river by the pavilion, and Barden Moor behind. A little further, keep straight on (the right branch) at a fork for the track to begin a steady pull towards the heights. As height is gained the intake wall returns, and at another fork (Intake farm drive) your route takes the initially less appealing way to the right. This green track soon perks up to head straight on as a similar track comes in from the right, now entirely amid heather. Down to the left are a handful of fields encircling Intake Farm, while the rocky crown of Simon's Seat looms to the north. Keep on through a gate in a fence, after which a track climbs from the farm to briefly join your track: take no notice as it quickly resumes its climb to the right. Your route now begins a cautious drop towards Pickles Gill Beck, reaching the stream at an old stone sheepfold in a setting that begs a halt.

Across the ford the path makes a short, steep climb onto Hazlewood Moor before easing out to undulate along to reach a junction. At 1115ft/340m, this is the highest point of the walk: the view includes Beamsley Beacon, Ilkley Moor, the South Pennines, Boulsworth Hill, Pendle Hill, Longridge Fell and the Bowland moors. Also, in view is the priory on the green valley floor. Just to your right a bilberry-roofed luncheon hut sits amid scattered gritstone boulders, a good refreshment halt as it's all downhill from here. Go down to the left to quickly reach Hammerthorn Gate, meeting a harder track coming in from the right to leave the moor together. Continue down the stony track, through a reedy pasture then down through fields to the attractive farmhouse of Bolton Park. Passing to the right of the buildings its drive leads down to the Storiths-Barden road, with just the bridge to re-cross to finish.

Ascending onto Hazlewood Moor from Pickles Gill Beck

BOLTON ABBEY

4 miles
from Bolton Abbey

A riverside stroll in fine surrounds: central feature is Upper Wharfedale's most famous building

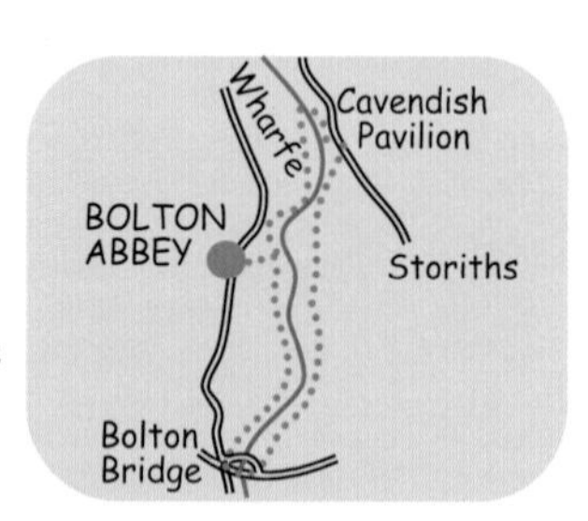

Start *Village centre (GR: 071539), car park*
Map *OS Explorer OL2, Yorkshire Dales South/West or Explorer 297, Lower Wharfedale/Washburn Valley*

Bolton Abbey is, strictly, the name for the tiny village whose showpiece is more correctly the Priory. It has Post office, shop, tearooms, bookshop, WC and a large, splendid example of a tithe barn. From the car park return to the road and cross to the 'Hole in the Wall', through which descend to the lovely environs of the priory. The imposing ruin dates from 1154, built by Augustinian canons. At the Dissolution the nave was spared, and remains to this day the parish church. Much else of interest in the vicinity includes adjacent Bolton Hall, dating from the 17th century.

On arriving at the wooden footbridge, don't cross but follow the Wharfe downstream. A long, pleasant pasture leads all the way to Bolton Bridge. As it appears ahead, there is an option to strike right to the Devonshire Arms. At the end of the pasture join the old road at the shapely bridge, left in peace on completion of the 1994 by-pass. A steam railway from Embsay sees Bolton Abbey station back in use, along the A59 towards Skipton. Cross the bridge, and beyond a cottage turn left on an enclosed path before Red Lion Farm, to enter a riverside pasture. As the Wharfe is neared the grassy way is deflected above a steep, wooded bank, and at the end it drops back down on a short-lived track to cross long, flat pastures parallel with the river. After a tiny stream and kissing-gate a wooded bank intervenes. A steep field is climbed, remaining with the fence to reach kissing-gates at the end, and a high-level vantage point which reveals the priory ruins in style.

Just beyond is a path junction where a snicket descends from Storiths. The main path slants down the bank to a T-junction where the right branch is followed: alternatively, remain on the bank top as a nice, thin path runs on the wallside to meet the ascending main one. Simply follow this on a grand high-level course along the top of the wooded bank, noting more than one decaying trunk embedded with coins. At the end it emerges onto a narrow road to ford Pickles Beck: a footbridge hides upstream. On the other side a stile/gate gives access to a riverbank path for the short stroll to a wooden bridge crossing to the Cavendish Pavilion.

The pavilion offers refreshments, with giftshop and WC alongside. Turn downstream to follow the bank of the Wharfe past the car park. At the end a path goes on through a kissing-gate, then with the priory just across the river, it swings right to climb to a gate and steps onto the road at the extravagant Cavendish Memorial. This recalls Lord Frederick Cavendish, assassinated in Phoenix Park, Dublin in 1882 (Cavendish is the family name of the Dukes of Devonshire, long-time owners of the Bolton Abbey estate). Turn left for a couple of minutes (with gorgeous views) to a gate into the priory grounds to enjoy further exploration.

Bolton Bridge

18 AROUND BEAMSLEY

3¼ miles
from Bolton Abbey

A delightful riverbank leads to an ancient bridge and Beamsley's wealth of interesting features

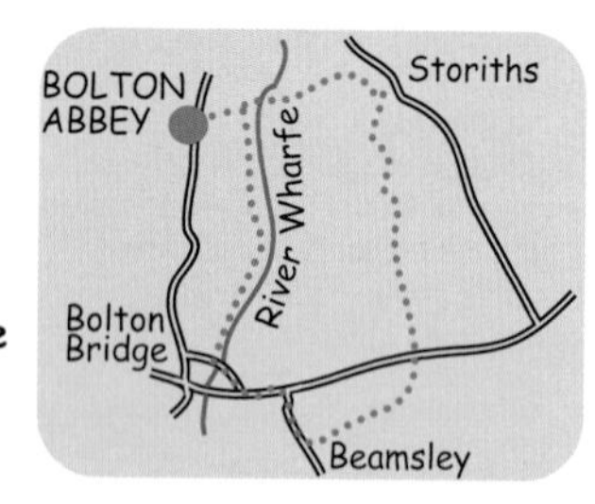

Start Village centre (GR: 071539), car park
Map OS Explorer OL2, Yorkshire Dales South/West or Explorer 297, Lower Wharfedale/Washburn Valley

From the car park return to the road and cross to the 'Hole in the Wall', through which descend to the lovely environs of the priory ruins - see page 40. Saving a look round for the end, go to the wooden footbridge, but without crossing follow the Wharfe downstream. A long, pleasant pasture leads all the way to Bolton Bridge. As it appears ahead, there is an option to strike right to the Devonshire Arms. At the end of the pasture join the old road at the shapely bridge, finally left in peace on completion of the 1994 by-pass. A steam railway from Embsay has seen Bolton Abbey's station back in use, a long half-mile along the A59 towards Skipton. Cross the bridge and remain on the old road to meet the A59.

Advance a short way along and cross with care to turn right into the scattered settlement of Beamsley. Before reaching the old mill turn opposite a Victorian postbox into Hardy Grange Farm. Go right of the buildings to a gate and stile ahead, with a drained millpond on the right. While the gate leads to a rough lane, the inviting stile sends a path alongside a drained mill-cut. Emerging into a field, make for a wall-stile in the far corner by some barns. With a simple weir on Kex Beck, an archway carries wall and path over the cut. Take the path upstream a short way to a gorse bank, then rise left with the wall to a hidden, tumbledown stile/gate. Head away with the wall, through another stile and along to a gate back onto the main road. Cross to reach Beamsley Hospital opposite. Through an arch, a second archway flanked by six almshouses reveals the roundhouse. From a central chapel seven individual rooms radiate: it now operates as a holiday let. A tablet in the main archway beneath the Clifford arms tells its origins:

This almshouse was founded by that excellent lady Margaret Russell Countess of Cumberland, wife to George Clifford, third Earl of Cumberland 1593, and was more perfectly finished by her only child Lady Anne Clifford, now Countess Dowager of Pembrooke, Dorsett and Montgomery. God's name be praised.

Back outside, a path rises past the postbox to a section of old road. A rough road goes back sharp left between houses to lead to New Hall Farm. Approaching it the path is diverted right along a wallside, then along from the corner to a small gate in a fence. Cross to a wall-stile ahead, then left across a small enclosure to the lower of two wall-stiles. Cross to a stile ahead, then slant up to the far end of the field. From a stile follow the right-hand wall, through a stile at the end to rise to another onto a lane in Storiths. On the back road up to the right is Back 'o th' Hill Farm with its refreshments and model railway. Your finish, however, is straight across to the farm opposite, passing left and down a short track to a small gate. This accesses a pleasant walled snicket to the wooded bank opposite the priory. Take the continuing path slanting down the bank, then left to the footbridge back to the ruins.

The Roundhouse, Beamsley Hospital

19 HAZLEWOOD & STORITHS

4½ miles
from Hazlewood

Rich variety in and above the side valley of Kex Beck, with a grand moorland finish

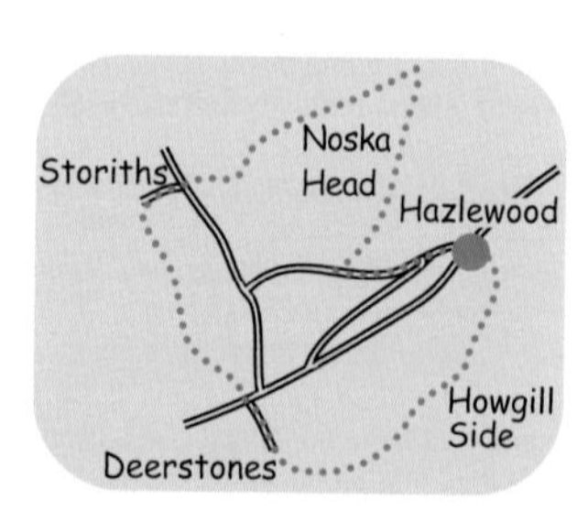

Start Hill End (GR: 094540), lay-by on old road off A59 (200 yards below a popular snack bar lay-by on main road)
Map OS Explorer OL2, Yorkshire Dales South/West or Explorer 297, Lower Wharfedale/Washburn Valley
Access Open Access land, no dogs: see page 5

Return to the main road and cross with care to embrace the colourful valley of Kex Beck beneath Beamsley Beacon. From a gate a surfaced track transforms into a green way dropping to a gate accessing a footbridge on the beck. Turning downstream a thin path enters new tree plantings, and is quickly deflected to rise with a wall to Low Howgill. Follow the drive out above Howgill Side and on to Ling Chapel Farm, with Beamsley Beacon's bouldery edge high above. Emerging onto open moor, turn right to cross the farm drive and down to a fence-gate. A grassy path descends the reedy moor, and through a small gate slants delectably down through colourful terrain into the steep-sided environs of Kex Beck.

Across a footbridge a thin path slants up to the houses at Deerstones. Bear right at the top to a gateway from where their access road rises back to the A59. Using a traffic island to cross, go left a few strides to leave by a gate. Head away with the wall to a stile at the far end. Continue along three further fieldsides then as the wall turns off, bear left to a ladder-stile ahead. Open views look across the valley to Barden Moor. Continue left to a stile defended by a stream crossed by stepping-stones. Head away with the wall now on your right, to the very end where a stile awaits. Continue with a wall on your right to a stile at the end, then rise to another onto a lane in Storiths. Turn right up to the back road through the hamlet. Just along to the left is Back o'th' Hill Farm with refreshments and a model railway.

Across the road is the pocket moor of Storiths Crag. Go straight across and head off on a short-lived track past a cottage. It quickly narrows to a path to rise up a wallside to meet a driveway. Turn left on this to approach Town End Farm, but then bear right onto the open moor. Grand views look over a splendid section of the Wharfe at the Cavendish Pavilion. Initially with the intake wall below, keep right at a fork for the track to begin a steady pull. Outspread now are the moorland flanks of Earl Seat and Hazlewood Moor. As height is gained the wall returns, and at another fork your route takes the initially less appealing way rising right through the heather. Simon's Seat's rocky tors are now seen over to the left. This green track soon improves, and after levelling out onto the brow of Noska Head, meets a lesser track coming in from the right.

Double back to the right on this for a grand, level stride with Beamsley Beacon increasingly prominent ahead. The track gently drops to a gate off the moor alongside the house at Witchey. Continue out along its access road between wide-spaced walls and through a pocket moor before slanting down onto the back road through the hamlet of Hazlewood. Turn left, passing the old school with its inscribed tablet of 1832. This traffic-free lane meets the old road just before the end.

The old school, Hazlewood

20 BEAMSLEY BEACON

4½ miles
from Beamsley

A perfect mini-mountain gives striking views over a hugely colourful landscape

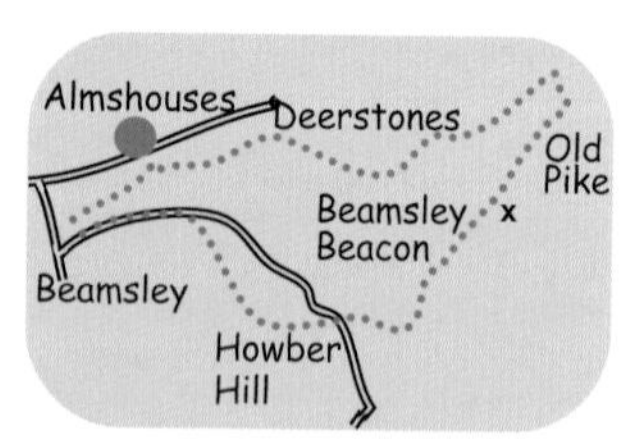

Start *Beamsley Hospital (GR: 082530), parking on section of old road by almshouses, or just a little higher off A59*
Map *OS Explorer 297, Lower Wharfedale/Washburn Valley*
Access *Open Access land: see page 5*

For a note on Beamsley Hospital see page 43. Cross the main road and from a small gate opposite head down two fields to a tumbledown stile/gate at the bottom, overlooking Kex Beck. A path drops through gorse, from where double back downstream to a barn at an old weir. The path squeezes between beck and wall to cross a footbridge. A little path ascends to a stile, then across to one in a wall. In open country, briefly follow the path right before a branch slants up the bank onto the road on the edge of Beamsley.

Go left, Beamsley Beacon appearing massive high above! After an enclosed spell the road swings uphill, here make use of a parallel path on the right. Levelling out to rejoin the road, cross a cattle-grid and bear right to a corner gate. Don't follow the drive but ascend by the wall to a gate at the top. Rise to a stile above, then bear right of Gibbeter Farm: over a wall-stile, on through a gap-stile then rising to a step-stile followed by a stile over a deer fence into new plantings at Wardla Hill. A good little path rises steeply away, easing out to another ladder-stile out of the wood. Cross to a wall-stile ahead, and faced with the houses at Howber Hill turn left on the drive back out onto the road at a parking area.

Cross to a wallside track onto the moor. When it quickly swings left take the wallside path right, and as the wall levels out it continues climbing to join another path on a brow. Turn left, at once forking left to enjoy a splendid ascent through heather above a bouldery edge. It abates to reveal Beamsley Beacon's summit ahead, and the path soon gains it. A cairn at 1296ft/395m on the beacon mound overlooks an OS column: the magnificent moorland panorama is secondary to the detailed view over today's agenda. The path continues on the crest to slightly higher Old Pike, its 1312ft/400m top marked by a shelter among a group of rocks in the heather.

A short pathless stretch follows: drop left to approach a crumbling wall, and go left to its junction with a sturdy wall. Just beyond this ignore the wall as it starts to drop away, in favour of a clear, level path. It rapidly forms a sunken way to begin a gentle slant across the fell beneath the Beacon. When the wall below turns sharply downhill, break off the now fading way and turn to descend moor-grass on the right: a quad track near the wall drops towards Ling Chapel Farm. Joining a drive, cross both this and the farm drive below to a gate in a fence. A grassy path descends the reedy moor, and through a small gate begins a delectable slant down into the colourful, steep-sided environs of Kex Beck.

Across a footbridge a thin path slants up to Deerstones. At the first house take a gate to its left, and a splendid green path runs by a wall overlooking the colourful ravine. The path then slants down to the beck, but on gaining it, leaves by a stile in front. The faint way resumes along the field edge outside the tree-lined beck, through a gate/stile at the end and narrowing to the point where you gained the beck at the start. Slant back up the modest bank to the tumbledown stile and retrace steps up the couple of fields.

Looking north from Beamsley Beacon